WITHDRAWN

EXPLORING THE WORLD

CABOT

John Cabot and the Journey to Newfoundland

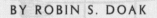

BY ROBIN S. DOAK

Content Adviser: Len Travers, Ph.D., Department of History,
University of Massachusetts, Dartmouth, Massachusetts

Reading Adviser: Dr. Linda D. Labbo, Department of Reading Education,
College of Education, The University of Georgia

COMPASS POINT BOOKS
MINNEAPOLIS, MINNESOTA

Compass Point Books
3109 West 50th Street, #115
Minneapolis, MN 55410

Visit Compass Point Books on the Internet at *www.compasspointbooks.com* or
e-mail your request to *custserv@compasspointbooks.com*

Photographs ©: Corbis, cover, 1; North Wind Picture Archives, back cover (background), 9, 10, 14, 15,
17, 38; www.canadianheritage.ca, ID #10086, Carlo Barrera Pezzi, National Archives of Canada, 4;
Giraudon/Art Resource, N.Y., 5; Scala/Art Resource, N.Y., 7, 37; Cameraphoto–Arte/Art Resource, N. Y., 8;
Stapleton Collection/Corbis, 11, 34; Stock Montage, 12, 32; Jose Fuste Raga/Corbis, 13; Chris Bland/Eye
Ubiquitous/Corbis, 16; Raymond Gehman/Corbis, 19, 28; Bettmann/Corbis, 20, 23, 31; Hulton/Archive by
Getty Images, 21, 39; John Farmar/Cordaiy Photo Library Ltd./Corbis, 22; Yann Arthus-Bertrand/Corbis,
25; Paul A. Souders/Corbis, 27; Drawing by A. S. Warren for Ballou's Pictorial Drawing-Room Companion,
April 7, 1855, from Charles de Volpi, Newfoundland; a Pictorial Record (Sherbrooke, Quebec: Longman
Canada Limited), 29; Tom Bean/Corbis, 30; Robert Estall/Corbis, 33; Werner Forman/Corbis, 35; Michael
Freeman/Corbis, 40.

Editors: E. Russell Primm, Emily J. Dolbear, Melissa McDaniel, and Catherine Neitge
Photo Researcher: Svetlana Zhurkina
Photo Selector: Linda S. Koutris
Designer: The Design Lab
Cartographer: XNR Productions, Inc.

Library of Congress Cataloging-in-Publication Data
Doak, Robin S. (Robin Santos), 1963–
  Cabot : John Cabot and the journey to Newfoundland / by Robin S. Doak.
     p. cm.— (Exploring the world)
Includes bibliographical references and index.
Contents: Man of mystery—A life on the sea—In King Henry's service— Setting sail for Asia—The New
World—A hero's welcome—To sea for the last time.
  ISBN 0-7565-0420-1 (hardcover)
  1. Cabot, John, d. 1498?—Juvenile literature. 2. America—Discovery and exploration—English—
Juvenile literature. 3. Explorers—America—Biography—Juvenile literature. 4. Explorers—Great
Britain—Biography—Juvenile literature. 5. Explorers—Italy—Biography—Juvenile literature. [1. Cabot,
John, d. 1498? 2. Explorers. 3. America—Discovery and exploration—English.] I. Title. II. Series.
  E129.C1 D66 2003
   970.01'7'092—dc21   2002009921

Table of Contents

NOTE: In this book, words that are defined in the glossary
are in **bold** the first time they appear in the text.

Man of Mystery

Who was John Cabot? What did he look like? What happened during his **voyages?** For more than five hundred years, **historians** have searched for answers to these and other questions about this great explorer. John Cabot is one of history's most mysterious adventurers. Many of the most important events of his life were not written down. The exact date and place of his birth are unknown. Little is known of his voyages. Even where and how Cabot died remains a mystery.

No **logs,** journals, maps, or charts from Cabot's journeys exist today. To get information about Cabot, historians have used letters written by people who lived at the same time. Some of these letters mention Cabot and his voyages. It is

John Cabot is famous for his exploration of North America, but many details about his life remain a mystery.

Christopher Columbus, another Italian explorer who searched for a direct route to Asia

known that Cabot was born in Italy around the same time as the explorer Christopher Columbus. Like Columbus, Cabot searched for a direct route to the spice **markets** of Asia. Like Columbus, Cabot found new lands that had

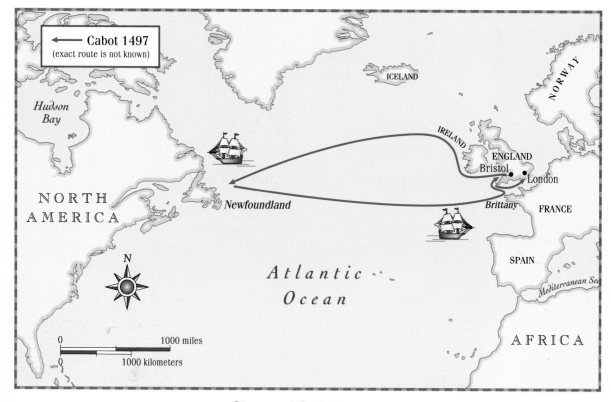

A map of Cabot's voyage

never been mapped. Both explorers believed they had reached Asia. They were wrong.

Unlike Columbus, Cabot was forgotten over the years. One of his journeys, however, was a **milestone** in exploration. Cabot was the first European to lay claim to the North American mainland. It was an area that he called the "New Founde Land."

A Life on the Sea

John Cabot was born Giovanni Caboto around 1450. Cabot was probably born in Genoa. It was a **city-state** on the Mediterranean Sea in what is now northwestern Italy. During the 1400s, Genoa was a busy seaport. It was one of the most important trading centers in Italy.

A view of Genoa, Italy, during the 1400s

The busy seaport of Venice

Around 1461, the Cabot family moved to Venice, another Italian city-state. Located on the Adriatic Sea, Venice was even bigger and busier than Genoa. Its port was the most important in all of Europe.

In the 1400s, **Venetian** merchants controlled the trade in goods from the Far East—places such as China and Japan. The merchants did not get their goods directly from the Far East, however. Instead, they bought spices, perfumes, silk, and other items from traders in Tunisia, Egypt, and Turkey. This area was known as the Middle East. These traders would not tell the merchants where they got such precious items.

After the Venetian merchants brought the spices

A merchant and camels carrying precious goods from the East

The silk made by these Chinese craftswomen would have sold for a high price in Europe in Cabot's time.

and other goods back to Venice, they sold them throughout Europe to make money. As a result, the price of spices and other goods from the Far East was very high.

Growing up in Venice, Cabot learned about sailing and the sea. Over the years, he spent a lot of time on ships. He became known as an excellent sailor. Cabot also learned about the spice trade from his father, who was a merchant. Cabot may have traveled to Mecca, in what is now Saudi Arabia. At that time, Mecca was the greatest trading center in the

Middle East. While in Mecca, Cabot would have learned that many spices came from the Far East.

Cabot began to think of ways to get rich from what he had learned. By leaving out the Middle Eastern traders, Cabot and other Venetian merchants could make even more money. Cabot decided to get the spices and other valuable goods from the Far East himself.

At that time, Europeans did not know about North and South America. Cabot believed

Maps such as this one reveal how European explorers viewed the world.

Sebastian Cabot, one of John's sons and another famous Italian explorer

that if he sailed west from Europe, he would get to Asia. He thought that the trip would be the shortest if he first sailed north and then headed west. Once Cabot got to Asia, he thought that he could easily sail south to Japan and China.

Around 1482, Cabot married a Venetian woman named Mattea. The couple had three sons—Ludovico, Sebastiano, and Sancio. The three boys all sailed with their father. They learned about the sea and trading. Later, Sebastiano became famous as the explorer Sebastian Cabot.

Cabot moved his family to Valencia, Spain, around 1490. At that time, the kingdoms of Spain and Portugal were interested in sending explorers to find the riches of the Far East.

Modern-day Valencia

Vasco da Gama was one of the explorers that Portugal would send to find a route to Asia.

Cabot may have thought that one of these two kingdoms would give him money for such a trip.

Both Spain and Portugal, however, had already paid for trips by other explorers. In 1493, Christopher Columbus returned to Spain after discovering what he incorrectly thought was a westward route to Asia. During his trip, Columbus had claimed new lands for Spain. Around the same time, the Portuguese were exploring a route to the Far East around the tip of Africa. Neither kingdom was interested in Cabot's plans.

Cabot needed to find someone willing to give him a chance. He began to consider King Henry VII of England. Henry became king in 1485. He wanted to turn his country into a strong European power.

King Henry VII of England

In King Henry's Service

By 1495, John Cabot and his family had settled in Bristol, England. Bristol was one of England's busiest ports. Wool, fish, wine, spices, and other goods from around Europe

Modern-day Bristol

Cabot discussed his plans for the voyage with English merchants.

were shipped into Bristol.

Cabot's decision to settle in Bristol made sense. The city faced west onto the Atlantic Ocean. That made it the perfect starting point for Cabot's voyage. Also, Bristol merchants were interested in Cabot's plans.

Beginning in the early 1480s, these merchants had paid for voyages into the North Atlantic Ocean. Some historians believe that ships from Bristol may have reached Canada even before Cabot got there. No written record of such a voyage exists, however.

The merchants may have been searching for new routes to Asia's spice markets. They may have been trying to discover the Isle of Hy Brasile. Hy Brasile was a **mythical** island that was thought to lie somewhere off the western coast of Ireland. The belief in Hy Brasile was so strong that the island was shown on a number of maps made around this time.

The merchants also may have been looking for fish. Cod was a popular food in England. The English had been getting their cod from Iceland, a country northwest of England. In the 1470s, however, English merchants and fishermen were not allowed to take fish from Iceland's waters. This meant that England needed its own fishing waters.

King Henry VII of England was ready to listen to Cabot's plans for a new route to Asia. When Christopher Columbus was trying to raise money for his trip, King Henry had said no. Now, with news of Columbus's success spreading throughout Europe, the king wanted to hear Cabot's plans. He wanted to make sure that England got its share of any newly found lands.

On March 5, 1496, King Henry gave Cabot permission to "sayle to all partes, countreys and seas, of the East, of the

The English needed to find fishing grounds other than those off Iceland.

West, and of the North." The king did not give Cabot permission to sail south. He did not want to cause problems with the Spanish. Because of Columbus's voyage, Spain had claimed the southern Atlantic area.

John Cabot (kneeling) convinced Henry VII to finance his exploration.

King Henry also gave Cabot permission to take control of any land he discovered. In return, King Henry demanded that he get one-fifth of all profits from these new lands.

Cabot finally had the chance to test his idea about a new route to the Far East. He also had the support of Bristol's merchants. The merchants agreed to pay for Cabot's trip. They promised to supply him with a ship and a crew.

Setting Sail for Asia

Cabot may have tried a first voyage in 1496. In December 1497, an English merchant named John Day wrote a letter to a Spaniard whom he called "Lord Grand **Admiral**." The Spaniard was not named in the letter, but some historians believe he was Christopher Columbus. In the letter, Day told about Cabot's journeys. He talked about a 1496 voyage and said, "He went with one ship, his crew confused him, he was short of supplies and ran into bad weather, and he decided to turn back."

Christopher Columbus may have been the "Lord Grand Admiral" to whom John Day wrote his letter.

A replica of the ship Matthew

Despite the first failed trip, Cabot did not want to give up. The Bristol merchants did not want to give up either. They agreed to pay for his next trip. The king had told Cabot to take

John Cabot (right) and his son Sebastian (behind him) before their departure from Bristol

five ships on his voyage, but the merchants gave him just one. Cabot called it the *Matthew.* The *Matthew* was a small wooden ship less than 70 feet (21 meters) long. It had three masts and a raised front and rear deck.

In the spring of 1497, Cabot loaded the *Matthew* with enough supplies to last for seven or eight months. Then, sometime during May, Cabot and his crew of eighteen or twenty men set sail from Bristol. The crew included a barber from Genoa, a Frenchman, two Bristol merchants, and some Bristol sailors. Many years later, Cabot's son Sebastian claimed to have been on board, too.

From Bristol, the *Matthew* sailed to the southern coast of Ireland. Cabot steered his ship north, following the western coast of Ireland. Then Cabot headed away from the coast and out into the ocean. His plan was to sail west until he reached the coast of Asia. It would be nearly a month until Cabot and his crew saw land again.

The exact route that Cabot took on this voyage is unknown. Cabot probably kept a log during his journey. He may have made maps and charts. Other men on board also may have kept journals or written letters about the trip. No firsthand accounts exist, however. All that is known about the trip comes from letters that other people wrote after it was over.

For most of the voyage, the ship sailed northwest, away from Europe. As the *Matthew* traveled through the cold Atlantic waters, it may have drifted a little to the south.

For part of the voyage, Cabot traveled along the Irish coast.

The New Founde Land

The *Matthew* enjoyed smooth sailing early in the voyage. The weather was pleasant, and the journey was uneventful. In June, however, Cabot and his crew faced a number of terrible storms. After the storms, the captain saw birds and pieces of floating wood. These were the first signs of land.

On the morning of June 24, 1497, the *Matthew* reached North America. Cabot was thrilled. He believed that he had reached an island off the coast of Asia and that he had found a faster route to the East. Cabot named the area he had discovered the "New Founde Land." Today, the island of Newfoundland still carries this name. It is the easternmost part of Canada.

Cabot's journey was a milestone in the history of exploration. His was the first known European sighting of North America since the year 986. That year, a Viking merchant named Bjarni Herjolfsson spotted the area after his ship was blown off course. Around 1000, Vikings

The shores of Newfoundland

led by Leif Eriksson explored the region. For a short time, the Vikings even established a settlement at the northern tip of Newfoundland.

Cabot went ashore to claim his newfound land for King Henry VII of England. The exact site of Cabot's landing is unknown. He may have landed somewhere on Newfoundland. Some people believe he may have landed farther south, on Cape Breton Island or Nova Scotia. A few historians think that Cabot might have landed as far south as Maine.

A trail exists today that marks the path he may have followed if he landed on Cape Breton Island. Onshore, Cabot met no one, but he did see signs of human life. He reported fields that had been cleared for planting and paths into the forests. Cabot also found some animal traps and a needle used to make nets. He took these back to the *Matthew*.

A path along the west side of Cape Breton known as the Cabot Trail marks one of the possible routes the explorer may have followed.

John Cabot plants a flag on North American soil.

He wanted to show them to the king when the ship returned to England. Before he left, Cabot placed a cross, an English flag, and a Venetian flag into the ground.

During the next weeks, the *Matthew* explored the coast. Again, no records exist that show exactly where Cabot sailed during this time. Later, Cabot would tell people in

Cabot noted that North American forests were filled with trees for shipbuilding.

England about the land he had seen. He would talk about the region's mild **climate.** He also saw grassy fields and forests filled with tall trees. The explorer noted that these trees were the same kind used in Europe for shipbuilding.

Cabot did not dis-cover any traces of silk or spices. He and his men found something, however, that would prove just as impor-tant: fish. The waters off the coast of the newfound land were full of cod! The fish were so plentiful, it was said, that Cabot's crew caught them simply by dipping baskets into the water. When they pulled the baskets back out, they were filled with fish.

Cabot realized how valuable North American lumber would be in English shipbuilding.

As the *Matthew* set sail for home, Cabot probably believed that his journey had been a success. He thought he had reached northeastern Asia. He believed he had discovered rich

*Cabot's crew reported that North
American waters were rich in fish.*

fishing waters, which would
please the merchants in
Bristol. Cabot was sure that
they would be willing to pay
for another voyage. He was
also certain that he would find
the riches he was looking for
on his next voyage.

A Hero's Welcome

Cabot's return trip to Europe took about fifteen days. The *Matthew* landed first at Brittany, a region in France not far from England. Then the ship turned north and headed back to Bristol.

Around August 6, Cabot and his crew sailed into Bristol to a hero's welcome. Cabot—and everyone else in Europe—believed that he had found a short, westward route to Asia. The discovery was one of the

A beach in Brittany

most important events of
1497. It made Cabot famous.
A Venetian living in London
said that in England, Cabot
"is called the Great Admiral,
great honour being paid to him,
and he goes dressed in silk."

After meeting with the
Bristol merchants who had paid
for his trip, Cabot hurried to
London. The king was waiting.

On August 10, Cabot met
with King Henry. He told the
king that he had reached
northeastern Asia. He told
King Henry about the mild
climate, the rich land, and the
waters full of fish. Cabot also
told the king that on his next
voyage, he would find the

GADUS MORHUA.
Der Kabeljau.
La Morue.
The Cod Fish.

Though Cabot did not return to England with Asian spices or silk, he did tell Henry VII of the plentiful fish he encountered on his voyage.

wealth that surely awaited.

King Henry was delighted. He gave Cabot a cash reward for his discovery. He also promised him a yearly income.

By the end of August, Cabot was back home in Bristol. He would not stay there long. He had already begun to plan a bigger, better voyage to the new lands he had discovered. First, he would return to the region he had found. From the New Founde Land, he would sail west to Japan. In Japan,

Cabot still hoped to find Eastern treasures, like this silk, on his second voyage.

Cabot planned to set up a trading post and begin sending valuable goods from Asia back to England.

To Sea for the Last Time

In the spring of 1498, all of Bristol looked forward to Cabot's next voyage. This trip would be much grander than the last. Cabot now led a fleet of five ships. One was paid for by the king. The other four were paid for by Bristol's merchants.

In May 1498, Cabot and between two hundred and three hundred men set sail from Bristol. Soon after, one of the ships returned to Ireland. It had been damaged in a storm. The other four ships sailed on and disappeared forever.

What happened to John Cabot and his men remains a mystery. In the early 1500s, one historian claimed that Cabot and his ships were lost at sea. Some believe that Cabot was shipwrecked off the rocky coast of Newfoundland. At Grates Cove on the northern tip of the island, later explorers found silver Venetian earrings and a broken Italian sword. This led some to believe that Cabot and his son Sancio were shipwrecked nearby. If so, they may have starved to death or been killed by native people in the area.

Some believe the ship may have run out of supplies. Perhaps the freezing cold and lack of food caused the crew to **mutiny** somewhere off the coast of Greenland. Others think that Cabot or one of his ships sailed south to the

An Italian sword like this one and a few other artifacts made people think that Cabot and his son died in Newfoundland.

The Spanish settlement of Hispaniola in the Caribbean

Caribbean Sea. That region was controlled by Spain, and Cabot's men may have been taken captive by the Spanish. Still others say that one or more of the ships explored the area, and then returned home. Cabot may have been among those to return. His yearly salary, given to him by King Henry, was paid once in 1499. Like other mysteries about

Many mysteries remain about the final voyage of John Cabot, depicted in this statue with his son Sebastian.

Cabot, there are no clear answers to the questions of

Cabot's exploration identified North American waters
as valuable fishing grounds, which they remain today.

how and when he died.

It seems that John Cabot and his voyages will remain a mystery. There is little information about him. Despite this, his achievements still rank him among the world's greatest explorers.

Cabot's explorations had a great effect on the course of history. His 1497 voyage opened up the North Atlantic fishing waters. It also influenced settlement in North America. After Cabot's final voyage, it must have been clear that Cabot had not found an easy route to Asia. People in England and all of Europe soon realized that what Cabot had discovered was a new **continent.** More than a hundred years would pass before the English began settling North America. Even then, they used Cabot's 1497 voyage to claim the continent. Over time, their settlements in North America would become an important part of England's vast **empire.**

Glossary

admiral—a high-ranking seaman

city-state—a city that is independent and is not part of a country

climate—the usual weather in a place

continent—one of the seven large landmasses of Earth

empire—a group of countries that have the same ruler

historians—people who study past events

logs—written records kept by the captain of a ship

markets—places where people buy and sell certain kinds of goods

milestone—an important event or development

mutiny—rebellion against a ship's captain

mythical—imaginary or not real

Venetian—of or from Venice, Italy

voyages—long journeys by sea

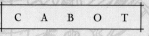

Did You Know?

❧ Some historians believe that the *Matthew* was named after John Cabot's wife, Mattea.

❧ After Cabot's first voyage for Henry VII, the king rewarded the explorer with what would currently be equal to about $15! The king would have been more pleased if Cabot had returned with Asian silk and spices.

❧ After his father's disappearance, Sebastian Cabot continued exploring. In 1525, he returned home from a Spanish expedition to South America with no riches and was banished to Africa for four years.

❧ A replica of the *Matthew* was built in 1996 in England. In 1997, the new ship traveled the same route as John Cabot did in 1497. It even had the same number of crew members and took the same amount of time for the voyage.

Important Dates in Cabot's Life

c. 1450
John Cabot
born in
Genoa, Italy

1485
Henry VII
becomes king
of England

c. 1461
The Cabot
family moves
to Venice

1492
Christopher
Columbus finds
what he incor-
rectly believes is
a westward route
to Asia, but what
is actually part of
the Americas

1495
Cabot moves
with his wife
and sons to
Bristol

1496
Henry VII gives
Cabot permis-
sion and money
to search for a
new route to
Asia

1497
Cabot sails the
Matthew out of Bristol
for his first voyage; a
few months later, he
claims Newfoundland
for Henry VII and
returns to England

1498
Cabot sets sail
from England on
his second voyage
but is never
heard from again

1499
Even though
Cabot has gone
missing, a yearly
salary given to
him by Henry VII
is mysteriously
marked as paid

Important People

SEBASTIAN CABOT (1484–1557) John Cabot's son and a famous mapmaker, he was also the first explorer to search for a Northwest Passage to Asia

CHRISTOPHER COLUMBUS (1451–1506) Italian explorer who sought a new trade route to Asia; he was among the first European explorers to set foot in America

JOHN DAY (?) English merchant who wrote a letter to a man many historians believe was Christopher Columbus, describing what was possibly an attempt at an early voyage by Cabot in 1496

LEIF ERIKSSON (c.980–c.1020) Viking explorer who landed on Newfoundland almost five hundred years before Cabot

HENRY VII (1457–1509) English king who gave John Cabot the money and ships to search for a new trade route to Asia

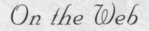
Want to Know More?

At the Library

Anthony, Laurence. *John Cabot.* New York: World Almanac Education, 2002.

Champion, Neil. *John Cabot.* Chicago: Heinemann Library, 2001.

Mattern, Joanne, and Patrick O'Brien. *The Travels of John and Sebastian Cabot.* Austin, Tex: Raintree/Steck-Vaughn, 2000.

On the Web

Biography and Picture
http://www.heritage.nf.ca/exploration/cabot.html
For helpful, in-depth information on John Cabot

Explorer Word Search
http://www.cbc4kids.ca/general/words/word-search/9812/default.html
For a puzzle to do online or print out, along with
short descriptions of explorers

John Cabot: Explorer
http://www.enchantedlearning.com/explorers/page/c/cabot.shtml
For a short biography of Cabot and a world map showing his routes

Matthew of Bristol
http://www.matthew.co.uk/
To look at a replica of Cabot's ship

Through the Mail

National Archives of Canada

395 Wellington Street
Ottawa, Ontario
K1A 0N3 Canada
866/578-7777
For all kinds of information about Canada's past

On the Road

The Cabot Trail

Cape Breton Highlands National Park
Ingonish Beach, Nova Scotia
B0C 1L0 Canada
902/224-2306
To visit the area that Cabot explored

Index

About the Author

Robin S. Doak has been writing for children for more than fourteen years. A former editor of *Weekly Reader* and *U*S*Kids* magazine, Ms. Doak has authored fun and educational materials for kids of all ages. Some of her work includes biographies of presidents such as John Tyler and Franklin D. Roosevelt, as well as other titles in this series. Ms. Doak is a past winner of an Educational Press Association of America Distinguished Achievement Award. She lives with her husband and three children in central Connecticut.